The Rerun

by Barry Brook

Copyright © by Harcourt Brace & Company

All rights reserved. No part of this publication may be reproduced or transmitted in any form or by any means, electronic or mechanical, including photocopy, recording, or any information storage and retrieval system, without permission in writing from the publisher.

Requests for permission to makes copies of any part of the work should be mailed : Permissions Department, Harcourt Brace & Company, 6277 Sea Harbor Drive, Orlando, FL 32887-6777.

HARCOURT BRACE and Quill Design is a registered trademark of Harcourt Brace & Company.

Printed in the United States of America

ISBN 0-15-313889-0

Ordering Options
ISBN 0-15-314003-8 (Grade 3 Collection)
ISBN 0-15-314098-4 (package of 5)

6 7 8 9 175 10 09 08 07

Matt and Cliff walked home from school. It was a Friday afternoon. The teachers never gave homework on Friday. The sun was shining. Things were looking good.

"Let's get our bikes and go to the comic book store," said Matt.

Cliff liked the idea. "I get my allowance today. We'll see if anything new came in."

"And I want to check out the baseball cards," added Matt.

 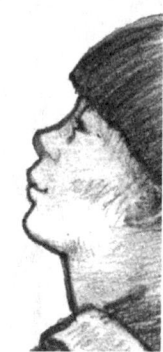

The boys turned the corner onto Lake Street. They saw brightly colored signs on the telephone poles. They ran to the first pole. The signs were for the county fair.

"Remember how great the rides were?" asked Matt.

"The Ferris wheel was the best," answered Cliff.

"I liked the whip," Matt added.

"Remember the relay race?" asked Cliff.

When Cliff spoke about the race, though, Matt's smile seemed to vanish.

"I remember we came in last. And it was my fault," said Matt. "I dropped the baton!"

"I didn't even think about that," said Cliff. "I just remembered how much fun it was. Let's ask Samantha and Susan if they'll be on our team again."

Matt wasn't at all sure he wanted to be in another relay race.

Matt couldn't forget what had happened last year. "We were leading," he said. "Samantha put the baton right in my hand . . ."

"And you dropped it," said Cliff. "It happens."

"I was so busy looking at the finish line that I didn't concentrate on the baton," Matt remembered.

"Then other runners came along. Someone kicked the baton. You couldn't even find it for a while," Cliff replied, grinning.

Matt didn't smile.

"We came in last."

"Matt, everyone makes mistakes. My dad says that's why they put erasers on pencils. So what do you think? Should we ask the girls?" asked Cliff.

"Okay," said Matt. He hoped the girls had forgotten his mistake. But he was afraid that Samantha would remember it and laugh at him.

"I like Samantha," said Matt. "But sometimes she's scary."

"What do you mean?" asked Cliff.

"Well, we both got an A in math," said Matt. "But my grade was a 95 and hers was a 98. She was so happy that she beat me. That bothered me."

"Susan's not like that," said Cliff.

"I know," said Matt. "Okay, you ask Samantha. I'll ask Susan."

"Sure," Cliff agreed.

When the boys arrived at Susan's house, both girls were sitting on the front steps.

"Are you going to the fair next week?" asked Matt.

"Of course," Samantha answered. "Isn't everyone?"

Cliff looked at Matt. Then he asked slowly, "Do you want to be on the relay team with us again?"

Matt looked like a sad puppy as he waited for the answer.

The two girls looked at each other. Susan was about to speak when Samantha jumped up.

"Only if Mr. Butterfingers puts glue all over his hand," she said.

Matt knew he could depend on Samantha to say something like that. And, most likely, she had more to say.

"Come on, Sam, we had fun last year," said Susan.

"Oh sure," replied Samantha. "It's really fun to be on a last-place team. Maybe we'll get a loser's medal."

Matt couldn't take any more. "We're going to win this time!" he shouted.

Matt surprised himself. He heard Samantha's sharp voice.

"Oh really? How's that going to happen?" she asked.

It took him a minute to answer. Could they really win? Then it came to him.

"Because this time we're going to *practice*," he said. His voice was strong.

The other kids looked at each other.

Then Cliff said, "No more jokes. No teasing. We're a team!"

The girls joined in. "You can depend on us. Let's start tomorrow!"

Matt was too excited to look at baseball cards now. "See you in the morning," he said.

The next day the team started early. They ran up and down the street. They passed the baton back and forth. When they dropped it, they tried again.

Samantha didn't tease. Matt didn't moan. Their team was good!

By Friday afternoon, they were better than good.

Saturday came. People crowded into the fair. There were dog and cat shows, horse shows, farm animals, and lots of food.

And, of course, there was the relay race.

As the runners were called to the starting line, Cliff shouted, "We're good!"

"No," yelled Samantha, "We're GREAT!"

The team huddled together and joined hands.

"Ready, team?" yelled Susan.

"Ready to win!" shouted Matt, Samantha, and Cliff.

And they did!

Running Facts

- Only men ran races in the Olympic Games in ancient Greece. Today, men and women run races in the Olympic Games, which take place every four years.

- The world's longest relay race took place in Melbourne, Australia in 1991. In that race, 23 members of a team ran 10,806 miles! It took them more than 50 days to finish.

- The largest track and field meet in the world takes place each year in Pennsylvania. Over 7,000 athletes compete in the games, called the Penn Relays.

TAKE-HOME BOOK